The Confidence Book
5 keys to self-confidence

Mark Stellar

Table of contents

Introduction

Self-confidence is elementary in any area of life we work in. We must believe in ourselves and have the possibilities to achieve what we strive to achieve. Whether we want to focus and study for a college degree, get the job of our dreams, or even get the love of our life.

If we don't have confidence in ourselves, if we don't develop the confidence, then it is common that we end up leaving it behind.

Unfortunately the environments in which we grow up are often not what we expect and instead of helping us to have security, what they do is plunge us into mistrust and can develop the ego, which is only a mask of what we fear inside.

Self-confidence is something we have to develop in order to increase self-confidence and self-esteem.

Imagine that you achieve what you like to do, or that you are capable of and have already done in the past, visualize that you can undertake long term goals and achieve them in a realistic way. The brain has the ability to imagine something in great detail if we focus on what we can do. If we prepare ourselves the brain will develop this and try it for the first time.

You have to work on silencing the inner voice that sabotages and says thath things can go wrong or that you can't achieve a certain goal. Imagine you have a remote control and you slowly turn it down to the type of voice of a comic carácter, like a cartoon character. This way, you can play down the negativity that is trying to undermine your security.

In this book we will go through everything that represents confidence and ego, how to learn to differentiate them and work on it to help you undertake what you propose.
You must sit more straight and upright, walk with poise, security, feel more confident in situations.
This is possible, no matter your current personality, no matter your fears, I will take you by the hand, showing you what each point means and in parallel I will tell you how to work to strengthen your confidence and get what you want.

Chapter 1: The Difference between Confidence and Ego

Let's start by knowing what confidence and ego are and then we'll see the difference between each of them. Let's start with confidence.

How to be more confident?

Self-confidence is feeling confident about yourself and your talent, not seen in an arrogant way, but in a realistic way. Security is not feeling superior to others; it is knowing, internally and with serenity, that one is a capable person.
A person who has confidence in himself is characterized by:

- Look confident before you look unconfident.

- He knows he can rely on his talents and skills to cope with whatever may happen.

- Feels prepared to face challenges every day, such as doing an important job interview or taking a test.

- First thinks "I can" before thinking "I can't"

What's so important about being confident?

Self-confidence helps us feel prepared to face life's experiences. When we have confidence in ourselves, we tend to approach people and create opportunities, we don't walk away from them if things don't work out at first, the lack of confidence in ourselves doesn't help us to try this again if we fail at first.

When a person does not have confidence, does not try new things, he may be afraid to talk to a stranger, even if this has a highly positive probability of improving his life.

Having a lack of confidence means that you can't go for the full potential that you have inside.

Believe in yourself

Stop for a moment and take a look back at your life, remember the moments when someone has told you that you are a smart person, that he has never met someone so smart for a certain thing. The times when someone told you that you were funny, kind, that you had talent for being an artist, a good student, a good writer, the best sportsman.

Anything positive they told you.

Those moments when we are praised or recognized for that talent we have, we are more confident, of course this is as long as we believe that and do not think they are mediocre people who think we are talented because we have a bit of talent. If others tell us this and recognize it, it is because they want us to see that we have talent and that they have affection for us in order to fill us with their words.

To feel confident, you have to truly believe that you are capable of achieving whatever you set out to do. The best way to develop this is to manage the belief and use talents or skills through learning and practice. Self-confidence helps to advance in discovering ourselves and developing our capabilities. When we see ourselves in this way, we feel capable and proud of our achievements, and the confidence we have becomes stronger.

How to gain self-confidence

Let's go ahead and see how to work on self-confidence, before we make the comparison with the ego. We all do things to gain more confidence. Consider these tips:

- Build an attitude of mental confidence: when the inner voice is telling you that it can't, or isn't able to, you can say, "I know I can learn or do such a thing if I pay full attention".

- You must be kind to yourself, when you compare yourself with others: it is common for us to compare ourselves with others, it is a way of understanding ourselves and developing the qualities we admire, but if the comparisons are to feel bad about yourself, they leave a bad taste and it is a sign that it is time to do something to improve and increase self-esteem.

- Doubts must be dispelled: when you doubt the skills you have, you get a feeling of inferiority, such as invalid, unworthy or unprepared, this can lead you to avoid people and situations that could help you grow.

- Low-risk actions: this is part of growing up, it can be being part of a volunteering, helping with a school project, participating in a show, being more involved in neighborhood meetings or at school, in summary, doing whatever boosts confidence and help us feel better without risks that have big consequences.

- Get out of the comfort zone: you have to choose something you want to do and give yourself that push with no excuses, without the assurance that it will work or come out well. Try it out and be surprised at what you can achieve.

- Recognize the talent you have and let it shine, they teach us to work hard to improve the weak points, but sometimes it is important to know the strong ones to know that we have to focus on those and try harder.

- Do the right thing: take on the commitments you have pending, don't fall into procrastination, prepare the classes, take the exams, the tests and keep up with the schoolwork. The best way to deal with anxiety about the challenges you have to face is to keep up with the pace and achieve what you set out to do.

- Show yourself: let others see who you are, with the mistakes, the insecurities and everything you own. It's easier to face your insecurities when you don't have to hide them. Accept the peculiarities instead of trying to like other people or acting in a way that is not your own.

This was briefly addressed here, but throughout the book I will be showing tools on how to face these conditions and make the best of them so that the confidence in you is solid and you achieve everything you set out to do.
Now that we have seen what confidence is and what you need to develop it, let's see what the ego is.

What is ego

You've probably heard the word "ego" in your life. You may know the meaning but, do you know what it really is and the influence it has on your life?
Perhaps in your life you have come across people who think they are always right, who don't listen and who defend their opinions above all circumstances. This attitude is one of the characteristics of people who have this excessive ego.
It can be with a boss or with a partner, a friend, or whoever. A person with whom it is impossible to reason, where his or her opinion is what matters.
Surely if you start thinking a little, you will find no problem remembering the faces and names of people and remembering situations lived with them.
Ego is Latin for "I". This for psychology is the psychic instance through which the individual recognizes himself and is aware of his own identity.

As a result, it mediates between reality, the ideals of the Overself and the instincts of the self. If we see it from the side of Freud's psychoanalysis, the id is composed of desires and impulses, the super-ego of morals and rules of society and the "I (ego)" is the balance that allows people to satisfy their needs while respecting the rules established by society.

Ego has to be controlled for health

In a study conducted at the University of Bradford in the United Kingdom, they concluded that 62% of people who believed they were right, were affected by stress and anger. All this ended up affecting their immune system.

Moreover, people who do not know how to control their ego and defend their opinion without listening to others, are often a source of problems with friends, family, partners, colleagues and everyone around them in their lives.

All this ends up generating isolation and damaging relationships with others.

Although careful, there is an ego that is positive. Let's look at it so that you can better understand the subject.

The Positive Ego

Having an ego isn't bad. We all have an ego, they work it very often in Yoga and meditation schools. When we learn to channel it is very useful and it is necessary that it comes accompanied by two vital elements, which is self-knowledge and emotional intelligence.

It is about us knowing the capacities and abilities and everything that affects us, it is also about us learning to listen to others, therefore the image of the ego is usually pejorative, but it is not so.

Is it good or bad to feed the ego?

Many people claim to love themselves, but what they really want is to have a real image of themselves. Nowadays, it is more common to pretend not only with people we know or care or love, but also with ourselves.

It happens that sometimes one hides one's fears, as well as insecurities, and makes a mask that diverts from what we really are. This is a wrong way to feed the ego, because others have unrealistic images of us. To feed the ego in a healthy way is to recognize the defects, the fears before us and before people, even if we feel vulnerable. We must remember that showing ourselves as we are requires courage, in order to have a good personal growth.

So, what are the differences between ego and confidence?

Maybe many people have thought that having confidence and quite a bit of ego is the same thing, they have already seen that it is not. It is normal to have this belief, because since childhood we are taught to look at others before ourselves and when you are an adult is described as self-centered looking at yourself and feeling confident. The point is that

there is a fine line between having a healthy ego and having an ego that becomes a mask to hide fears.
Sometimes it also happens that confidence is confused with the ego and the needs of others are put before our own and we seek external approval and feel guilty when we want to say no, but are forced to say yes so as not to remain selfish. The consequence of all this is the disconnection with our needs and we forget to listen to ourselves and therefore value ourselves as we deserve, this is why we are going to see the differences between security and ego to understand once and for all, this:

The admiration for oneself

A person who has a high ego, has great admiration for himself, so much so that he develops traits of narcissism and sees the world from a distorted angle. The problem is that these people believe themselves to be superior to others and consider themselves to be perfect, and what they do they see as well.
The problem with this is that they think they are perfect people and as I said before, they think only they do things right.
Now, when you have a secure personality, even though you have value of your own, you do it from a realistic point of view. It is aware of the virtues and defects and does not try to camouflage them to appear what it is not. He accepts them as they are and if one of them causes him problems he tries to find a solution.

There is nothing wrong with admiring oneself, loving oneself, saying positive things to oneself, the problem is believing oneself to be perfect and better than others. All people have defects and the fact of seeing them helps to work on improving them. Pretending not to have them is not good for us.

Caring for oneself and others

The difference between self-esteem and ego can be seen clearly at this point. Someone with an ego cares about himself, but never about others. He needs to be the center of attention, to catch the looks, and if this does not happen he feels that he is ignored and the reaction that appears is anger.
A person who has confidence in himself, cares for himself, but also for others. He knows how to listen and does not seek to be the center of attention. A person who has self-esteem knows what empathy means and has more enriching relationships.

Seeing beyond one's own beliefs

When dealing with a person who has a very high ego, the first thing you notice is that he is not able to see beyond his beliefs, it will be impossible to expect him to question them or to reflect on them. He believes that his vision is the only true one, and this generates many conflicts with others.

A person who has a high dose of self-esteem is able to look beyond the point of view. They know that the vision they have is not the only one and understand that others have different perspectives, they may even feel interested in them. The fact that they can listen, put themselves in someone else's shoes and gain a new perspective on a situation makes relationships healthier and more rewarding.

As you can see, there is a clear difference between the self-confident person and the person with an ego. The person with an ego does not generate empathy or put themselves in the other's shoes.

That requires a lot of self-confidence, but someone with an ego really does not care or respect, just covers and hides what he is not interested in, so it is difficult for them to see beyond.

The difficulty of accepting criticism

A person who has a lot of ego can't stand being told anything, he doesn't want his image to be damaged and what they are distorted. He has hidden his defects under the mask of grandiosity; anything that reveals it causes them to take up arms and become defensive, angry and blame others.

When someone is self-confident, they recognize their flaws and have no problem receiving criticism to help them be better. He does not take this as a bad thing, but appreciates it, now, as long as the criticisms are constructive and are not said with venom and bad faith.

You mature as a human being when you become self-critical and accept constructive criticism from others.

Expect to receive something in return

Throughout life we will meet people with a big ego who only think about themselves. So if they ever ask for help or come forward with some kind of interest, is because there is something that can benefit them.
If he does not achieve anything positive, the person with ego will not show interest. It does not act in a healthy way, it does not transmit anything good. But when working on one's self-confidence, one does not use others to achieve one's ends. Someone who has self-esteem is never driven by interest. When a person is self-confident, he is generous and does not think of the benefit of his relationships with others.

The hierarchy between people

Another of the great differences between self-confidence and ego is that the egomaniac believes himself to be above others. He may think this, either because he considers himself superior in strength, intelligence, beauty, power, whatever. He believes that the world revolves around them, they are the sun. A person who is self-confident knows that no person is superior to another, they are just different. That's why they don't make comparisons. It's like the egomaniac saying that a car mechanic doesn't know how to write as well as the egomaniac does, but the car mechanic will repair cars as the egomaniac will never do. We all have qualities and talents that others do not. That makes us different and unique.

To give first you have to give yourself

Another major difference between security and ego relates to the belief that we must first meet the needs of others before our own. However, we cannot give of that which we do not have.
A person with a large dose of ego cannot love healthily and cannot meet the needs of others if he has not met his own needs first. That is why life goes on after constant attempts to appear, to camouflage and to believe oneself to be the best of all.This does not happen with people who have a self-confidence, they respect themselves, accept what they are, value themselves and love themselves, so they are able to have enriching relationships, learn what they need and then give themselves to others.
We have all fallen into the clutches of the ego, but this can not make us feel guilty, we have to see it head on and allow us to realize that it hides something behind the problems of self-esteem.

Chapter 2: Changing Limiting Beliefs

Limiting beliefs prevent us from moving towards what we want to achieve in life. We all want to achieve goals and for some reason that we don't understand, we get stuck.

This may be because of limiting beliefs. Let's get to know them and work on them so that they are not an impediment to moving forward.

What are limiting beliefs?

Limiting beliefs are a perception that we have of reality that prevents us from growing. We cannot develop as people or achieve the things that fill us with illusion. It is something that is not really true, but that the mind sees it that way and for us this is true and we take it for granted.

Maybe it is something that we have lived with since childhood, or was incorporated into our lives at some point through an experience or an opinion.

If you change your beliefs and attitude you will see that it will change everything around you. If you think you can't do it, your brain already predisposes you to it. Even if you are visualizing the future, naturally from the catastrophe part, and thinking that everything will go wrong instead of everything going right, then it will affect us in scenarios like:

Searching for a job:

You'll come up with phrases like: I'm not going to get a job that's interesting to me.
There must be a thousand candidates by now, and they're not going to pick me.
It's impossible for me to find a job but as it is, I'm sure I won't like it or I'll be underpaid.
I don't think I know how to do that, I'd better look for something less than that and they'll tell me yes, I'd better not waste time trying this. If I go into this business it will go wrong, that's for sure.
If you're talking about a new job or a promotion, you'll come up with phrases like:
I'm not up for that promotion or I'm not ready for that application yet, I'm not going to live up to that.
I don't deserve that raise, anyone can do better, not me.
When it's something related to the search for a partner, phrases like:
No one's gonna notice me, with my ugly, dumb, simple-minded, whatever I look like. I'd better not even try and I don't look ridiculous.
I won't go to that party, I'll have a hard time and I have no one to see there

All the girls who are worth it already hang out with better men than me, if I go they will make fun of me because I went, he is just there, they will say.

In the use of social networks and ICT:

This social networking is for young people now, me, at this age I'm going to be stupid in a network full of boys.

This handling of computers has been difficult for me and will be forever. I won't do it. No, I won't.

I'd like to sell my crafts online, but that's for young, talented people, not me doing this to de-stress.

All these refusals can be due to a single bad experience in the past and they apply it for life in all scenarios.

It can be the poetry reading where he went blank, the meeting where he was asked something and got stuck, some slip of a job, a failed attempt.

Then these phrases appear, like: they already made me see that I was useless, that's why I always miss.

This is like Jorge Bucay's story about the chained elephant: it is this elephant that when it was small was tied to a weak iron bar that was tied to the ground, it grows up in prison and when it grows up it doesn't understand that with a sigh from its trunk it can let go of that tie and be free.

Thus we go through life, tied to imaginary ropes.

Limiting beliefs can be changed because they are just that, chains. Many times someone thinks:

- Showing feelings is for weak people.

- I have to be hard at work to make myself respected by others.

- Whoever has money today is because they inherited it from the family or earned it by stealing.

- You can't trust people, everyone is on their own, you have to compete to win.

- I'm a failure..

Where beliefs are born

We human beings begin to build our beliefs with the model of reality that we have at the moment we are born. In childhood we discover the basic workings of the world and learn what is right and what is wrong.
Then, in our adolescence, we develop beliefs about who we are and how we relate to others.
After that, when we are young, we begin to come to conclusions about our purpose in life, career, or relationships.
The process continues indefinitely and today we continue to complete the model of reality and update it to the discoveries that appear and that we make.
We learn this in two ways.
The first is through our own experiences, that is, through what we live in the first person. Then we interact with the world and receive feedback and based on this we deduce how things work. It is like learning that if we stick our fingers in the socket we get a shock, the belief "sockets give current" is installed in us and is part of our reality.

Likewise, if every time you tell a joke people laugh, it doesn't take long to conclude that you're funny and that you're a joke maker.

This is the most direct and immediate way we have to know the truths and we use it constantly, however, it can't always be done, nor do we care to do it. This is why we have the ability to learn socially.

I invite you to think about these statements:

- If you throw yourself off a tenth floor you'll kill yourself.

- The earth is round (unless you are a flat-earth believer)

- Going out naked is not right.

These are conclusions that you have reached based on your personal experience in your life. Beliefs acquired from others, from parents, friends, teachers, but also from books, movies, TV ads. This is now part of your reality.

Therefore, thanks to the ability to learn socially, you learn from your own beliefs and you now have a map of how the world works and it helps you make decisions every day.

The problem is when this map has errors and you are taken out of the way.

The limitations of human learning

What happens is that beliefs are very powerful, even though they are only hypotheses about how reality is believed to work, the problem is why the brain sees them as absolute truths and acts as if they were real.

This is positive, positive because it allows you to solve many tasks and make decisions about them that you take on a daily basis. Although it is also a double-edged sword because if the model of reality is wrong, you will constantly make wrong decisions and worst of all: you will not realize it and think you are doing things right.

Unfortunately it is easy to end up accepting these wrong or limiting beliefs, because the two learning mechanisms used create the reality map and are far from perfect.

Let's look at the limitations of each:

First-hand experiences

When you deduce the functioning of the world by means of experiences, from there the own experiences happen. What you do is assume that the world will always behave in a particular way just because it has happened that way on other occasions. This is correct in some cases, for example, if you put your hand in the candle, you'll get burned, that will never change. But things are not as easy as this statement:

- You coach a football team and, for example, you get injured, it doesn't mean that every time you play you're going to get injured.

- If you approach a girl to talk to her and she rejects you, it's not that you're ugly and you're doomed to be alone all your life, there probably wasn't any feeling with her and that's it.

- If the boyfriend you had cheated on you, it's not because all men will. He didn't value you and one who does will come along.

Faced with such emotional situations, it is easy to rush in and think that we will get hurt, rejected or cheated on. Many assume this as reality and the bad thing is that they attract it, because they set the universe in motion to make it happen.

Now imagine a couple of smart kids alike, studying at the same school and in the same year, but in different groups.

The first kid gets an amazing math teacher, he's great at teaching, he does it with fun. He's demanding with the homework and makes sure everyone does the exercises and understands them so they're ready for the test. This child learns and passes with an A. Then based on this he adds two beliefs:

- Math is fun.

- I'm good at numbers.

The other child, on the other hand, has to be with a horrible teacher. He explains like he's in college, he's narrow-minded, he just dictates what's in the book and doesn't put in a little pedagogy to make it fun. He never gives homework and never watches how the youngsters are doing, except when he fails them in their exams.

This second child fails and his parents make him take private lessons in the summer, they punish him for not learning and based on this the child adds a couple of beliefs that many of us have about the subject:

- Math is boring.

- I'm not good at numbers.

If you've noticed, this concludes that both kids have the same skills and goals, but one sees math as horrible and the other sees it as great to be able to do so much with numbers.
Maybe neither of them will go away to work on subjects that involve numbers and both will be successful at what they do. But the point is that beliefs have a profound impact on the subject of math, on grades, and on the career they choose. Maybe one of them will study Social Communication, where they don't give math, and the other will choose anything because he has no problem with numbers. Belief has its role there.

Socialization

Human beings are often analyzing what others are saying and using the information to build or adjust the model of reality we have.
When we are young, we need to learn fast, so we take for granted whatever we see and hear. But as we grow up we become more selective and begin to evaluate ideas that come to us from the outside by three criteria:

- The credibility of that idea and its source.

- How well the idea fits into the model of reality we have.

- The number of people who believe that reality is true.

When we see that the idea comes from someone who is credible, who fits that model we have at that moment and that there are those who support it, we take it as true.

One example is that if you ask a very close friend who constantly participates in swimming, how to do the butterfly stroke, you will hear all the advice he gives you. His source is credible because of the experience, the affection for the friend and the background you have of his personality. You will assume that many follow this model.

Now, if you see a stranger on the street looking bad, announcing the end of the world, you will ignore him because he has no credibility and because he says something that makes no sense. But even if he had people around him, you wouldn't believe him because he doesn't meet the criteria.

Usually the filter we have on ideas works well for us, but sometimes it has its flaws, for various reasons:

- The most credible sources can also be wrong.

- Just because something makes sense doesn't mean it's true.

- Just because people believe or do something doesn't mean it's right.

This is why some people still believe that eating more than 5 eggs a week is bad for your health.
If you look at this, you will see that it meets the criteria we saw earlier:

- You learned it from a credible source like a parent, doctor or nutritionist.

- It makes sense because eggs have cholesterol and too much cholesterol is dangerous, so eating eggs may not be recommended, you think.

- Many people support the idea and you just have to google it to see what they say and see that belief established.

But it's not true at all that eating five eggs a week is bad. It's just a model of reality that many people have.

How to build a more reliable reality model

You can see then, that it is very simple to add wrong beliefs to the model of reality and it is something that happens without you even realizing it. What's more, it's even inevitable.
As a child, you're going to believe what your parents tell you and what they tell you at school, this without questioning the truth. You don't have a choice.

However, now that you are an adult and have the ability to think for yourself, you must use the power of the conscious mind to distinguish what is true and what is not. In this way you will build the most reliable and accurate model of reality. Consider these tips:

Be careful when you identify the causes of what has happened

When something happens that directly affects or draws attention to you, the first thing you do is try to identify the cause of what happened. This may seem simple, it is not always so, but if you rush into one of the fallacies of questionable cause, you can conclude that the event is only for a cause when in fact it was not.

To avoid this, you have to get used to asking yourself these questions:

- Is this the real cause of what has happened, or are these just facts that are related to something in the past?

- Is this the real cause of what has happened or does my mind take me to that moment in the past?

- Is this the only cause or might there be more causes that I don't take into account?

If you fail to identify the cause of an event, you will inevitably draw the wrong conclusions from it so you are likely to mess this up.

Don't forget how complex the world is

Don't go jumping to conclusions about what you're going through. Because they're usually wrong or incomplete at best.
Just because a person has taken advantage of you when you were nice to them doesn't always mean that the same thing will happen later or that the project has gone wrong doesn't mean that you are useless.
The world is full of probabilities, so don't rely on beliefs of "if I do A, B always happens" or "as X happened, I am a Y". This is rarely true.

You must be aware that others are wrong

Many times when we evaluate a situation, a source comes to mind that we take for granted, for example, parents, experts, or someone we admire and take this for granted.
The problem here is that everyone, even the wise and the Nobel Prize winners, make mistakes, and if we listen to what these trusted people tell us we run the risk of ending up believing something wrong and that it is not beneficial to us.
Credibility increases the chances of ideas, whether they are right or wrong, but it does not guarantee it. That's why when it comes to important things it's not a bad idea to corroborate the veracity of the idea with other reliable sources before integrating it into the model of reality.

Don't forget that others have their own goals

Every day you will come across people and institutions interested in you believing some things and behaving in such a way, to check this, just turn on the TV or open a magazine and analyze the advertising.
If you look, you will realize that the objective of advertisers is that you associate having a product with positive qualities and feelings and not having it with negative qualities and feelings.
The reason?
They know that if they can convince you that if you drink such a brand of soda you are happy person, you will be happy to drink it. If you put on such a brand of deodorant, women will run excitedly to you. All these advertisements lead you to buy and act like them.
Of course, none of these messages are true and companies are aware of this, yet they use them constantly because it works for them.
This is a phenomenon that is not only seen in advertising, but in other sources that are taken as credible: the famous scientific studies.
Many media do not aim to get closer to the truth, but to change people's model of reality so that they act in a certain way.
For this reason, when you evaluate someone else's idea, always ask yourself
What interest can that person have in me believing what they say?
If you see a hidden motive for this, then analyze it in great detail.

Think rationally

It's common to accept an idea as true, just because we feel it's real, or because we think that's how things work.
You have to learn to analyze ideas in a rational way, use logic to see if things are true or not, look for data and objective facts to form an opinion about them.
Although this doesn't mean you have to completely ignore intuition, intuition is a useful tool when it comes to making decisions and building a model of the world and assessing what is true and what is false.

Think for yourself

This is another piece of advice you need to keep in mind when dealing with limiting beliefs. Think for yourself, don't believe something is true just because there are many people who believe it too. Nor because I say so.
You have to ask yourself if this is true, history has constantly shown that society can be wrong and that everyone considered universal truths, they were not in fact.
There are only a few brave people who dared to question the popular wisdom and confront the status quo and because of that they uncovered the error and moved us forward as a species. Stop following the herd and think for yourself.
The world is a complex place, to move in it without being blocked or going crazy, we store in our minds a simplified model of reality that allows us to make decisions and evaluate any fact quickly.

To build the model we use two sources of information, the experiences we live first hand and what others do and say. Generally our process works well. Sometimes we make mistakes and end up believing something that is not true.

This is not a problem because if the model of reality is wrong, you will make the wrong decisions. That's why it's important to always keep in mind what I shared with you in this chapter:

- Be careful when you identify the causes of things.

- Remember that the world is a complex place.

- Be aware that others make mistakes.

- Being aware of others also has its objectives.

- Think rationally.

- Think for yourself.

But even if you follow my advice to the letter, the model of reality will not always be perfect. You will carry with you incorrect, incomplete, or limiting beliefs.

Since your beliefs form the reality model and the reality model determines the results, you should constantly update your beliefs and replace them with more beneficial ones.

Unfortunately, changing beliefs for others is not easy, it's like saying: now I'm going to believe this instead of what I believed before.

Beliefs live in our subconscious and the process is more complex. But it is still possible to change what you believe and you notice that when you set out to do so.

Positive mental reprogramming

There are many techniques that exist to make a mental programming that is successful for us. The idea is to choose the one or the ones that are aligned with oneself, in which we feel identified and that can be used daily.
Constancy is part of the pillars of success in mental programming. It has to be done in order to progress and what better way to do this than being able to do it anywhere.

The Daily Self Support

In this you can fill your soul and do the reprogramming by writing daily notes where you are filled with good messages, for example you can say:

- I want to get better.

- I want to achieve success.

- I want to have peace of mind in my life.

In the morning, when you wake up take a card, look at it for a while, close your eyes, look at yourself as if you were looking at a mirror, visualize well, with success, feel the tranquility and improvement. Then mentally repeat the sentence with a pause:

- I'll do very well today.

- I will be successful and calm on this day.

- Everything will be better, much better.

At night, when you go to sleep, look at the card and repeat the phrase, ten times:
- Tomorrow I'll do very well.

- I will be successful and peaceful.

- I will feel good, very good, tomorrow.

The ideal here is that you see it as achieved and to repeat it mentally, when you do it, you reinforce the idea from the conscious allowing the subconscious to accept it as valid and mobilize beyond time and space. In this way it happens.

The Visualization

To visualize is to see with your eyes closed, it is to see events from the near future of the near or distant future as if it were done now. It's seeing the clearest and most real thing if we're sick. It is seeing us well, successfully at work or in the place of study.
To visualize is to project the mental screen, it is to watch a movie of something you want to do.

If you think you don't know how to visualize or you've never done it, look at it this way. Observe an object in detail, close your eyes and look at it, visualize it with all its details. The next day, remember the image, close your eyes and visualize it again, try to reproduce it mentally in the most exact way possible. Then compare it with the real object observed the day before, analyze errors in the visualization and what you failed to remember. Close your eyes and visualize the object again.

Setting Goals

To be able to do things you have to have goals to achieve. They have to be logical goals that are within our reach. There is a saying that if you are a glass, do not pretend to be a golden cup. But you do have to strive to be the best glass.

The first thing is that you set goals that you want to achieve, then write them down in a prominent way on the card and look at this card every day, seeing it as achieved and channeling the strength towards the goal set, thinking positively that the goal can be achieved by repeating self-supporting phrases that reinforce towards success.

It is a goal for a student to want to finish school well. For the working person, it is a goal to want to be well at work or to want one. What is important is not where you are, but the direction you take. The mental attitude that is established and the direction that we decide to take. The man becomes what he thinks, to help us to have goals and approach them by contemplating the ideal we want to achieve.

The Positive Reminder

The experts recommend that we have one or several cards, on one side we put the X signs that are positive, that add up and on the other side we put the letters PMA.

When you look at the card it reminds you that with a positive mental attitude, that is PMA, you multiply X with the latent positives that we all have.

You can have it at your workplace or in your studio and seeing it every now and then is special to do when you are going through a difficult time.

Just looking at the card reminds us that having a positive mental attitude at that moment, we will face the problem better and manage to solve it favorably.

Chapter 3: Developing Skills to Build Safety

The most common answer you get to the question of what is the longing you have in this life is for people to say that they want to get to have permanent happiness. Happiness is very much related to self-confidence. Therefore, being a confident and fearless person, valuing what life has to offer, being guided by values and being coherent with what one is, is the path that will lead to happiness.

How I become a confident person

One of the most important components in life's outcomes is the habits we have. Habits are powerful factors that influence what happens to us. Since they are solid and often unconscious patterns that repeat themselves constantly and daily, they influence life and do not always or only do good.

The good thing here is that habits can be changed, new ones can be learned and we can leave behind what does not help us feel better or reach our goals, this requires effort and commitment to ourselves in order to achieve it.

Let's look at those habits as power skills to deploy and move towards goals in a safe way.

Let's look at the skills that are needed to achieve that balance and personal well-being and thus have better self-confidence.

Ability to be proactive

A person who has proactive behavior is a person who acts before a future situation occurs rather than just reacting to events. This means that he or she takes control and makes things happen instead of just adjusting to the situation or waiting for something to happen.

Ability to start things off knowing what we're doing them for

This skill develops and gives meaning to ideas and life. It allows the project to be oriented towards what is valuable to us.

Ability to prioritize what is really important

It allows us to discern between what is urgent and what is important and to dedicate time to what gives value to life, is the ability to convert ideas into reality.

Ability to use win-win thinking

It is the ability to develop a thought that makes us question the need that, for me to win another has to lose, and that life is a zero-sum game, changing it to the concept that you can win - win.

Ability to understand before being understood

From a position of respect for others and empathy first, we can then be understood. This is the key to good human relations and to having a win-win agreement.

Ability to search for synergies

One plus one equals three, as the saying goes. This is the skill where diversity is valued in any life environment. It's being aware of the result of working together with people of different ideas. It is greater than the sum of each element or each part and acting in isolation.

Ability to work on your personal development

It is to use one's capacity to renew oneself and grow constantly in one's conception of oneself and of the world. It is achieving balance between the different roles that one has in life.

Look for incentives that make you feel good about your work

It's important to feel good at work. If you don't have a job now, you can do volunteer work to help improve your personal confidence.

Full attention or mindfulness

With full attention, one can pay attention and be present using techniques such as meditation and yoga.
It has been shown to help people become more aware of their thoughts, making them easier to manage.

Don't try to be perfect

That of perfection does not exist, it is a lie, do not seek to please everyone because this is impossible. Do not be good at everything because you will not stand out in anything. Don't try to take responsibility because you'll end up psychologically broken. Be flexible.

Read a book

With the books you open a window to other worlds, other characters, you see other points of view that will fill you as a person and make you see life differently. A book is like psychotherapy.

Change your look if necessary

Take a bath, go to the hairdresser's and buy new clothes. Just changing the look is effective.
Wash every day, use a new shade of lipstick or do something different with your hair or clothes, then don't hesitate to smile at yourself in the mirror before sharing that smile with others.
Watch your body posture, keep your head up, shoulders back and walk with confidence.

Don't turn to drugs to feel better

This also includes tobacco and alcoholic beverages. If you learn to fight without resorting to these escapes, the confidence in you will increase considerably.
To face life you don't need shortcuts or anything like that because in the end life will take its toll on you and it will be fat and hard to pay.

Don't compare yourself to others

Common mistake. Many people compare themselves to others and feel bad. There are some who compare themselves to TV stars. Comparisons can make you feel miserable. Using them as inspiration is one thing, but not pretending to be identical to them.

Make a list of your achievements

Write down each one of them: if you can cook, read books, play sports, write. That thing you take for granted that you can do and like. If you are a good paid person, if you take care of the children's education, if you are a loyal friend. It is easy to forget what we have achieved in life.

Make a list of your positive inner qualities

Write down if you are a good person, if you consider others, if you enjoy the gift of patience, if you are intelligent, funny, reliable, supportive. All of that, write it down.
Check this list often to encourage you in critical moments.

Being your own best friend

If you're such a good friend to others, why don't be one for yourself. If your best friend is having a bad day, you could go and help him out.
That's what you should do for yourself. Lend a hand, think about it. You'll see that you'll be kinder, more understanding. It's a wonderful thing, being supportive. Be better about yourself from now on.

Learning self-defense

Learning self-defense helps increase personal confidence. This has been proven and is said by many schools of martial arts. It is that self-confidence is the perception or consideration that we have of ourselves as individual beings.

It is that valuation, respect and recognition of our own capabilities. When security is healthy, one thinks with motivation and in a positive way. It leads to taking the reins of destiny and trusting in who we are as a person. Many situations affect destiny, trusting what we are as a person.

But many situations can affect us and make us feel weak, vulnerable and less valuable.It can be bullying at school or work or living with toxic individuals or couples that can ruin personal safety. It can be bullying at school or work or living with toxic individuals or couples that can ruin personal safety. Likewise, having received psychological threats, assaults or attacks of some kind can ruin our perception.

Other factors such as routine, daily commitments, stress, anxiety, and social interrelationships trigger stagnation that can lead to the belief that we are worth less or that we don't outgrow ourselves. There are many ways to break this vicious circle and one way is for us to learn how to defend ourselves, gain strength and know how to act in a conscious way when faced with hypothetical or risky situations.

Mastering the art of self-defense does not imply years of study and many hours of exercise. Nor is it a field where only men go. On the contrary, many women resort to this art to safeguard their integrity and life. Women have the morphology and psychological skills to be great at self-defense, being precise and forceful. If we see what the body can do, it is evident that self-defense helps to stay flexible, relaxed, and with a better weight. If we work we feel better about ourselves and this is another part of the reward.

The best thing here is that you learn protection and it does not require much effort, the goal is to provide some tool that is easy to apply, that is adapted to the size and build, age, physical disadvantages or fragility of the person.

Keep in mind that there are several types of self-defence to start with and you should know where to choose. There is karate, boxing, krav Maga and a wide variety more. There are some where in just three months you can get out of potentially risky situations. Even if you feel like Jet Li or Lucy Liu, after taking these classes, it is important that you know that the purpose of them is to increase your self-confidence and the possibilities of escaping from the aggressors. Finally, remember that:

- It helps you work your body, from your arms, legs and buttocks. There is not a part that does not receive benefits from the art of self-defense.

- You burn calories and have fun, because you can burn up to 2000 calories in 90 minutes. The body will appreciate this. You can define your silhouette and see positive changes before three months.

- You feel better about yourself. If it gives you a lot of confidence, security and balance, for psychological, physical and spiritual well-being, from the first day you will see changes and you will not want to miss anything.

Finally, there is nothing better than living without fear. Learning to defend yourself helps you to detect weaknesses in yourself and in your opponent, as well as it helps you to keep control at all times.

Learning to dance

Dancing is another method that serves to increase one's self-confidence. It is one of the best gifts you can give yourself. Dance is art, it is a tool to express intimate feelings with the movements you give your body. It is a great strategy to develop a positive and kind vision of yourself.
There is a wide range and varied dances and they all imply many benefits for human beings of any age. Both for emotional well-being and physical health. It improves self-esteem and this is one of those benefits that stands out the most.
Those who take the step to learn to dance, struggle with a fear that is ingrained in everyone, that of making a fool of themselves, adhere to the freedom of expressing the self without fear and with more security.
It is true that not all dances are suitable for everyone, but if you want to dance to improve your security, depending on your personality and body, you will choose a freer or more disciplined style.

In this way, the therapeutic benefits are achieved. Dance is a discipline that integrates itself into various aspects of the human being, which is vital for self-esteem and psychic well-being.

There is a connection with three parts of the human body. Dancing is a dose of creativity that requires the use of both hemispheres of the brain. It stimulates the intimate and personal energy that flows from the soul, from the depths of the emotions. It is an integral experience that serves to confront the main obstacles to good personal security: shame, self-criticism and negative thinking.

It helps to improve the relationship with the body. Dancing is a way to feel more at ease, it is a means to express emotions and it does not matter the proportions nor the shape, neither the size, some styles of dance are the joy of the body, of any body, for example, belly dancing, salsa, African dances or flamenco, styles that help with personal image.

You achieve a liberation of the self. You develop creativity in an undeniable way and with dance you have a chance to free yourself and be yourself. If you look at the dancers, you will see that each one dances with his own essence.

You develop self-confidence. When you learn to dance you have a great adventure with many rewards that generate an immense amount of positive emotions. Each dance class is a new learning experience and is overcoming obstacles that help in a positive way in the self-confidence. Dancing is a therapy to improve self-esteem and confidence.

The dance is mindfulness

We live in a society with people who care about what happened today and what will happen tomorrow. We cannot disconnect from the present moment. Dancing is about focusing on music in the dances in the exercises and there is no intrusive thought while dancing. This is a great exercise for the mind and helps to have control over the emotions of the day. This helps to bring out the self-confidence and ideas that put you in danger.

Finally, dancing helps to improve social skills. Personal confidence is related to social relationships, because of the intrinsic nature of it. One of the most social activities is dancing. Going to classes is the best way to meet people and have a pleasant social life.It is an activity that nurtures security, you don't need a partner to enjoy ballroom dancing, as you see, dancing improves your self-confidence and it is very easy, it is just to get into a dance academy, go to a place where you like to dance and start to dance with others and learn a new experience.

Chapter 4: Improve your personal image

Consciously or unconsciously we transmit what we are and the vision through the way we dress, speak, the way we move.

Since ancient civilizations, the way we dress has had an effect on professions and trades as well as on social status. Personal image reflects our education, personality, behaviour and state of mind. The personal image is composed of two aspects which are the internal image or self-image and the external image which is the one we project to the outside.

The internal image is the way we see ourselves, and it has to work from self-evaluation, improving self-esteem and accepting unconditionally who we are.

On the other hand, the external image is the one that reflects through clothing, accessories, hairstyle, posture and the way we speak and behave. Many times we work only on the external image and become slaves of fashion, forgetting the most important thing which is how we feel about ourselves.

The power of the personal image is in connecting our internal image with the external one, to achieve this it is necessary to resort to creative visualization.

Improve the inner image to convey it to the outside

This can be achieved through creative visualization. This is the ability to imagine an idea through a mental image, to build what we want, that is, how the imagination functions and how it can be driven to work for us as a tool for transforming dreams, desires and goals into reality.

With creative visualization you can have a high positive impact on life, if we are aware of the focus we give to thoughts, we are what we think and sooner or later what we think will be reflected in our lives.

Thoughts are energy, they are vibrations that repeat themselves in time and model the present now and the future to come. You must ensure that the thoughts have quality, to be built in positive, to bring everything we want in our lives.

I invite you to follow this to improve the image you have from within, you achieve it with the incredible creative visualization:

- Place yourself in a quiet place, use your favorite place in the house, a place where you can relax and know that no one is going to interrupt you.

- Prepare the space, light an incense or a candle to harmonize the atmosphere.

- Make yourself comfortable, get ready to visualize, sit or lie down in a position so that you will be comfortable for a while.

- Clear your mind, close your eyes take some deep breaths, clear your mind and relax.

- Visualize the goals and connect with what you feel: when you feel that you connect with the essence start to visualize, you can focus on a specific goal that you want to achieve and that relates to improving your personal image. The methodology can help not only with goals about personal image, but in general with any goal that you manifest. Create an image about what you want to manifest, for example if you want to lose weight, visualize yourself as someone happy, with the ideal weight, full of energy, with a lot of vitality. You have to be specific about the details. Imagine places, sounds, people, colors, aromas, flavors, everything that relates to the goal you want to achieve and connect with that and you will see that the path begins to build.

- Practice constantly. This process has as a main ingredient to practice a lot, as well as with the muscles that are exercised to tone them, the same happens with the mind, do the exercise for 21 days without stopping, so you feel that the habit settles in you, the time you will spend on each session depends on you. You can dedicate about fifteen minutes, or more, or less, you decide.

- When you have learned to use creative visualization in a conscious way, you can make great changes within yourself so that they manifest on the outside. Remember that imagination is everything; it is a preview of what is to come.

Use this technique daily and enjoy the incredible results and connect with the changes you want in your life.

Changing the external image

When we are in the process of transforming ourselves, we have to work on our outside. We all do. There is an essay by Myriam Rius that talks about tips to improve personal image and groups them into categories. Let's work on them. So that you can use them in your own transformation.
In the first category are grouped tips related to presence and physical appearance.

Take care of your appearance

The body image, the visual image that is offered, reinforces personal security, promotes social acceptance and confidence a priori. You must be aware of this at all times.
This is true, especially when one feels comfortable with oneself, this is transmitted to others and is perceived by everyone. It has nothing to do with size, ethnicity, size, natural beauty, it refers to general care. To how much we take care of ourselves.

Take special care of the details

Here it refers to personal care, hair, teeth, nails, breath. The way you look at yourself speaks to others and does so before you use words. In this sense, even the smallest detail is important.
At this point there is nothing much to say, it is something we generally agree on, we do not want communication noises, things as simple as dirty shoes, old ties, ugly nails, greasy and unkempt hair, everything damages the image for others and of course, for ourselves.

Making the most of what you have

Not all of us have been equally privileged by nature, the less privileged people take advantage of what they have. If you can't find a way to do it, go to a professional, there is more and more efficiency in good service. I am not entirely sure of the approach of this sentence, but it can be deduced that it refers to the fact that there is no such thing as an ungraceful person, but that he or she has not been fixed in the best way. This has nothing to do with natural beauty; we all have things to do with it. We should try to create a balance or visual equilibrium so that after the seven seconds of the first impression, a favorable environment for communication has been created.

Clothing

It must be appropriate to the occasion, the clothing is a symbol of belonging to a particular social or professional group and of distinction, status. It should be noted that the codes are not universal. They vary according to the time and the geographical location. The important thing is to know how to dress appropriately for the occasion, if you do not know the codes, then look or ask.

It is true that not all work environments have the same dress codes and as the phrase says, when in Rome, do as the romans. If you have doubts do not be afraid to ask, especially if you are starting in a new place or it is an event you have never been to before. Sometimes it is better to do a little research to be better dressed than to be worse off than others because of ignorance. Dress for the position you want, not the one you have now.

Avoid the enemies of the image

They are easily identified: the wrong size, damaged or unsuitable garments and accessories. These are common mistakes and many times we don't even know about them. It is better to leave the accessories if they are going to spoil the clean and neat look. Garments considered outdated are not usually very important, because in work or professional spaces fashion is not taken into consideration as much as the classic, elegant and sober. You can adapt fashion to your personal style with a few touches, but it's definitely not the main thing.

Get a better wardrobe

With the aim of always being well dressed in the same way, without breaking the bank. It especially has to do with women so that they can look better since they have much more variety. Changing the wardrobe is expensive, but you can have elementary clothes that go with everything and make you look much better.
In these cases we must, according to the budget, accommodate the wardrobe, for each season of the year.With garments that are basic, of very good quality, that can be used on several occasions and can be combined with each other. It is essential to know this.

Your stuff talks about you

The car, the cell phone, the paper you write on, all this stuff you have speaks of you. They talk about what you are.
How can a professional photographer who takes pictures with a cell phone be trusted?
The best image is of the photographer with his tripod, camera and all the photographic equipment. What you wear as a professional speaks volumes about you. You have to make sure they say what you want them to say.
I've seen this for a long time and it does have an influence, it's not just banality. We live in a world where you eat with your eyes and if we feel good about our surroundings, it reinforces security.

If you are looking for a professional to offer you a service, you would know that without having a lot of information about it, you would notice what he uses for work, how he looks like, both in terms of clothes and care, cleanliness, haircut and all this. All this will influence your decision making.

Prepare an Elevator Speech

Having a speech is part of improving one's external image and feeling safe. You must show yourself to be kind, agile, showing what you are, what you do. Looking for what you want to find, what you want or sell. Everything helps a lot to complete the image you project through the visual aspect. You must be able to adapt your speech to the speaker and to the specific moment so that you have the opportunity to pronounce it.

This is important when you have a point of contact with a client, with someone you want to relate to, with a possible partner. Be confident when you speak, the speech must show coherence, a pleasant thread because knowing how to speak clearly is something that fills you with confidence and makes you feel proud.

If you improve the image for a business, have business cards

Framed in the search of improving the image for a business you have to pay attention to other details, such as having business cards.

This improves the image they have of you as well as providing contact details to be located in the future. You should get used to carrying them around with you. Do not abuse them, do not offer them as if you were handing out leaflets. Hand them out at a networking event, when you detect that someone else wants to make contact with you.

If you work in a company, you only have to make sure that they are in good condition. If you are independent, look for a card that leaves a pleasant memory, so that when they think of you, the look of the card has made a good impact.

Practical tips to make an impact on others and be happy.

Believe it or not, image has a lot to do with happiness. Let's see.

- Stop thinking that image is something frivolous. Image determines a lot in your life. It influences your mood, your humor, your confidence and your self-confidence. It also influences your happiness. Image influences what others think of you, judge you, and value you for what the image says about you.

- Do not listen to those who defend that the external aspect is not important, that the beauty of people is within them. A good image opens doors in all areas of life. You will see that when you transform this aspect of your life will begin to open hundreds of doors that will invite you to other spaces not explored so far.

- Do not put the wishes, desires, needs of others as a couple, children, colleagues at work, to yours. Do not let the love of others override you. You are a special person as they are. With the same right to enjoy life and what makes you happ.

- Don't fool yourself into thinking that you don't care what others think of your appearance. You may feel that you don't care, but they don't. Remember a phrase that is very wise: how they see you, they treat yo.

- Don't obsess over your body's weaknesses and pay attention to the ones that make you proud. You may be a little overweight, a few inches shorter, wider hips, or smaller breasts. Don't forget the beautiful eyes you have, the lined legs, the marked waist or your beautiful hands.

- Don't think that a good image has to do with being tall and dark, blond, thin and with guitar curves. The world is full of people where their image is far from the archetype of beauty, but they are still handsome and irresistible.

- Don't hide behind lack of time because of children, work, age or weight to avoid enjoying that image. They are excuses that do not deceive anyone, least of all yourself. If you really want it, you'll find a way.

- Don't justify the careless image with the argument of naturalness. Being natural has nothing to do with being badly dressed, disheveled, or looking bad.

- Do not go beyond your appearance because no one will look. You deserve to look better for yourself. It's time for you to do for yourself what you would do for others.

- Don't link a good image to money anymore. There are many things you can do to improve your appearance that don't cost anything. It's just a matter of creativity and doing a little research.

- Don't be embarrassed to admit that you don't know what you can do to improve your image. To dress better or to have style. It's something you haven't been taught anywhere, it's something normal that like many other people, you haven't found the time.

- Don't think that comfort is a concept, it is something mental, there is no doubt that home slippers are the best footwear you can wear, but going out in the street will make you look bad. Sometimes you have to suffer to look good.

- Do not copy the styles of celebrities, maybe you do not have the body of those people or the face or hair, what feels to those people may not feel to you, then you will look badtrying to imitate a celebrity, which will detract from the strength of your personality, remember that you are unique.

- Stop adapting to trends and let them adapt to you. You can even quit if they don't favor you. You don't have to or need to take anything that is not good for you. You don't deserve that.

- Don't be so sorry and take action. Things don't change on their own.

Chapter 5: Becoming independent and the comfort zone

Independence is part of becoming a more confident person. Throughout life there are many stages that are important to us. Like when you are a child and have to distance yourself from your parents and when you enter adulthood. This makes it necessary and important that we manage to strengthen our own security. Everyone should know that they can manage on their own.

Getting out of your comfort zone

To get out of the comfort zone is to make difficult decisions, is that you have to do something with which there is no comfort, but that is precisely the idea, is to abandon that routine and face to overcome fears.

It may not be easy, but after you learn how to get out of your comfort zone and make the decision to do so, you feel a little fear and anxiety but in the end you feel the triumph of having achieved it.

When you do it, you feel like you're growing up. Moreover, successful people understand the importance of getting out of this comfort zone, they push themselves, break their limits and try new experiences and expand the power of the mind. Getting out of the comfort zone is about having clarity to achieve different results and it is about acting differently, even if it causes fear, it is about escaping from the routine that in the end looks like fun.

If you are wondering how to get out of your comfort zone, I'm going to show you a series of tips that will help you leave that comfort zone and start feeling really good.

Each one of the keys to get out of your comfort zone has the goal of getting you to break habits, get you out of context, increase your mental power and leave behind the limiting beliefs that have brought you to where you are today:

- Take a cold shower, it is scientifically proven that it wakes up the body and leaves it ready for action, a warm shower on the contrary relaxes you for the rest.

- Start the talking, connecting with 5 different people on the street.

- Wake up before the alarm sounds, get out and walk, grab a bike.

- If you order a drink at the bar, order an orange juice or an iced tea.

- Get out of something you don't use anymore like those old toys, those used notebooks, broken objects. Do it for thirty days.

- Change your route to work.

- Cook something and eat something new.

- Turn off the networks and mobile for a couple of days.

- Accept the following invitation from someone you haven't seen in a while.

- Learn something you don't like or think is useless. Learn a new language.

- Go out wearing something that draws attention on the street, something you'd never wear.

- Call someone and talk to him for a while. You'll like it.

- Get a new job, change your chair, consider other businesses, work online if you've never done it.

- When you buy something you look to pay less with discounts or promotions. Many countries have this culture, so it will not be difficult.

- Ask a stranger anything, like what day it is, you can even ask what year it is. It sounds crazy but it's a way to break that fear.

- Go to work on your bike.

- Check your finances and write down the five areas where you spend the most money. Start saving.

- Leave the house five minutes before your usual wake-up time. Make sure you do what you want on the condition that you stay out for 20 minutes.

- Install a camera and record the workday, look at it and analyze this as if you were someone else. Judge and implement what needs to be done to improve.

- Go to a new restaurant or bar you don't know instead of going to the usual place.

- If you spend the whole day at home, pack your lunch and spend the afternoon somewhere else, go coworking for a day, work in a mall with Wifi, do something you haven't done until now.

- Help a street person, give them something, take what you don't use to a foundation.

- When you see a stranger, you can wish him a great day. It may sound strange, but it's a way out of that comfort zone.

- Take a breath and try to conquer the biggest fears you have, like flying, snakes or any animal.

- If you live with your parents, take flight and face the fears of living alone and responsible for yourself, certainly another way out of the comfort zone.

- Move to another country, learn another language.

- Break that fear of public speaking, you can organize a talk or a lecture at any event, allow yourself to speak, prepare a speech and face the many pairs of eyes that look at you.

- Sometime when you have to go to an event and the director or manager asks for help, offer it immediately.

- If you have a vice, leave it for a week, like coffee, cigarettes, beer, gambling addiction, etc.

- If you don't have a partner, you can find someone to talk to, flirt with, and tell them what you like and why you like them.

- If you have an unoccupied room at home, rent it out and earn extra money as well as break the rhythm of your life.

- If you go on vacation, go to a hostel and share a room, it's a totally different experience that you may or may not love. But it is something that certainly takes you out of your comfort zone.

- Go somewhere public and look for people who share your tastes, sit down and enjoy the company.

- If you are learning something new, like a language for example, speak only this language for a week or as long as you can.

- Go for a run, this is the key to being smarter and having more memory. According to neuroscience studies.

- If you find it difficult, then sleep naked.

- Don't text for a week if you find it difficult, don't use your cell phone while driving, although you should leave it permanently. It's too dangerous to do that.

- Find a part-time job that is foreign to you and apply for it. You can earn extra money and it will serve as another source of income.

- Try reading a book on the bus or subway and leave the music aside.

All this and more is aimed at getting you to leave the place where you are, to activate you to go for more and get it. When you leave the comfort zone you feel safer, you consider yourself more capable of achieving whatever goal you set for yourself. I assure you that when you leave the comfort zone you will achieve more goals and you will grow as an individual.

Chapter 6: Fear of what others think

Many people around the world live with something called "fear of what others think". It's an anguish that they're going to be judged this way or that way. It is clear that we all need to be accepted but falling into this kind of thinking constantly, totally conditions our way of life.

Behind the focus is a lack in self-esteem. We can always feel more or less the restlessness about the opinion that can be given about us with those people who are important, but we must not lose the freedom and the essence that characterizes us.

What others will think is a shadow. It is a double-edged sword that we have always had. It is the one that puts up walls to the autonomy that slows down our steps and forces us to be careful not to break the implicit rules that assume that everything is fine.

There are many social scenarios that are impregnated with social prejudices that are not only seen in small towns. It is the restlessness that is always present in the workplace, even in the families themselves.

This is how you face the fear of what other people think

The fear of what other people say puts us in a state of eternal hypervigilance, it directs our attention to the external universe where conclusions are drawn, about what can happen to us.

It is a defensive analysis that feeds, that changes behaviors to adjust to what others expect. These are behaviors that are described in psychology and understood as interpretative bias. Moreover, one cannot leave out the bias that is directly linked to anxiety. There are several studies on this subject, such as the one carried out at Ultrech University by Dr. Elke Salemin, which demonstrates the relation. If we don't obsess over interpreting everything we see, hear or live, focusing on what they can say about us, then we feed the anxiety.

Overcoming the fear of rejection

If the happiness you have is blocked by the barrier of rejection, stop. Think about this for a moment and see if it's really worth it. If the fear you have is of being rejected, by family, friends or society, weigh the parts to see what weighs more heavily on your heart.
You can't be what you're not or hide forever your thoughts and desires. Pretending to be something you are not will one day bring out the frustration and low self-esteem.
It is not worth losing your personal balance. It comes first, as does psychological balance.

Not everyone will like you

Be clear from the start, not everyone will like you. This is impossible, it's even healthy to know. The fear of what they'll say is related to the need to fit in.
Each of us has a personality and criteria and a voice, if we do not fit in with others we set limits that do not match our identity.

We don't have to get along with selfish personalities that humiliate and destroy. Not getting along with others offers autonomy and respect for one's own scale of values. It is necessary and hygienic.

Likewise, there are aspects that have to be understood, the more insecure we are, the less clear our ideas are and the worse value they will have on us.

You have to define criteria, positions, you have to stand firm on values and defend yourself, well-developed personalities with strong self-esteem do not let themselves be defeated and are not afraid of what they will say..

Accept criticism, put aside the fear of what people will say

Being criticized is part of the dynamics of society, so you have to analyze it as what it is, another point of view and you have to respect it without dramatizing it. Each one of us has an approach to life, with those varied and diverse points of view we have to learn to live together, but without judging or going to extremes.

Defend your position

Maybe others impose their ideas on what you do, preach their own morals and social norms, on what is right or wrong, don't allow this. Defend your positions, ideas and needs, do not let yourself be defeated or undervalued, because when you lose your values you will be losing yourself.

Turn off and overcome this fear of what people will say, praise yourself, put yourself in a good position.

Act on your own principles

The idea applies in any environment, even when you go shopping and let people which came with you to influence you. You have to do what makes you feel good, what makes you happy in both small and large decisions. Because if you lose your voice little by little, there will come a time when you won't hear anything from yourself.
If you're wondering if this is worth it, it's not. You must claim your rights and say so out loud. Fear of what others say need never affect you.

Analyze and focus on your goals

Achieving goals is not something you do because you are lucky. Discipline and enthusiasm are key to achieving anything you set out to do.
You have to learn from your mistakes and not give up when your plans don't work out the way you want them to.
In order to achieve your goals and success, you have to know that you have to face complex tasks. Whether it is in the work place, in the sentimental or academic environment. It is important that you determine your objectives and work for them every day, it is the best way to achieve them, if you don't do it you will not have a reason that will lead you to overcome.

If you want to achieve your goals I leave you some advice that will be of high value to you.

Develop a conqueror mentality

Don't let the frustration get to you. The positive spirit helps you to overcome the problems that come your way and find better solutions. Pessimistic and negative attitudes don't motivate you to do anything but feel victimized and carry the blame.

Set goals

This will help you project the path, identify what you want to achieve and how you can do it. Set general goals for success and then set specific goals with big results and specific deadlines that will allow you to have a good plan of action.

You have to be disciplined

Discipline is elementary to achieve your goals, they will help you get closer to your objectives little by little and achieve what you want in your life.

Register new ideas

If you are focused on the objectives you will be filled with motivation and generate new ideas to achieve what you want. Put this into action.

Be nice to others

If you have a good attitude you will have a better relationship with other people. You have to be kind and sincere, take care of your appearance and the tone of your voice. Do not accept humiliation or allow others to take advantage of your good will.

Keep the enthusiasm

Even if there are days when goals seem unattainable, enthusiasm will keep you in the right track, this will give inspiration to others and give you the boost you need to succeed.

Don't give up

Enthusiasm has to be with you at all times, even when things go wrong. Don't let a frustrated attempt keep you from your goals, learn from the experience, identify mistakes and improve for other opportunities.

Focus on objectives

Day-to-day obligations can distract you and make you lose sight of your goals, so focus on what you want to achieve and keep it in mind.

Take care of yourself

Physical, emotional and spiritual well-being will give you the strength to follow your plans of action, even if you project yourself into the future, live in the present and enjoy everyday happiness.

Seize the day

Don't expect things to happen just like that, or that the good things are there to light your way. You have to forge your destiny and take constant steps towards that goal you want to reach.

Chapter 7: Extra Advice

Self-confidence, as you have seen, takes many forms, from the arrogance that is the ego, to being self-assured and not believing oneself to be better than others.
Keep in mind that being self-confident is a person who is honest, who does not mask his fears and who is unique in his way of being.
When you talk about confidence, there is one thing that is sure and that is that real people feel confident and have the advantage that they are able to make things happen.
If you think you can do it or you can't do it in both cases you are right.

Mentality had the ability to affect a person's ability to succeed. A recent study by the University of Melbourne showed that those who were confident had better salaries.

At the end of this book, I want to share some extra tips for confident people that you can also use and that will be very useful to keep in mind:

They get happiness within them

Happiness is a critical element of trust because to be safe you must be happy with what you do. People who find satisfaction in their accomplishments know that no matter what others say, you are never as bad or as good as others think.

They never judge

Self-confident people don't judge others because they know that everyone has something good to offer and don't need to demean someone to feel good about themselves. They know how limiting it is to compare yourself with others and how tiring it can be to spend time wondering if you are too good.

They never say yes unless they want to

In a University of California, San Francisco study, it was shown that it is easier to experience stress, fatigue and depression if it becomes difficult to say no. Confident people know that it is healthy to say no from time to time, and they have the self-confidence to make it clear why they say no.

They don't use phrases like "I don't think I can" or "I'm not sure," they say no for sure. They know that refusing to do so honors previous commitments and allows them to fulfill them with excellence.

They listen more than they talk

Safe people listen, they don't talk much because they have nothing to prove, they know that by paying attention to others they learn more. Instead of seeing their interactions as opportunities to prove themselves, they see them as tools to get closer to people.

They are accurate in speaking

It's rare to hear safe people use crutches like "this..., um, I think..." they're individuals who know it's hard to get people to listen to you if you can't speak with conviction.

They're looking for small victories

It is a type of individual that imposes itself, even when the efforts only produce small victories, the actions help to generate necessary receptors for the brain that is responsible for the sensations of reward and motivation. The increase in these receptors also increases the body's amount of testosterone which leads to the desire to overcome other challenges. When you have a series of victories the confidence is made to last longer.

They exercise

In research done at the Eastern Ontario Research Institute, it was found that people who exercise a couple of times a week feel more socially capable. They also have a better body image and higher self-esteem. The best thing is that this was not achieved with the physical changes that take time to be appreciated but with the immediate discharge of endorphins that result from this exercise.

They're not looking for attention

People walk away from those individuals who kill themselves to get attention, people who realize that the attitude passes quickly and appeals to them more than hearing from a few important people who know each other.
Self-confident people don't pretend to be the center of attention, when they get the looks of everyone for an achievement, they look for others to receive the same, the people who worked with them.

They're not afraid to err

They are people who are not afraid to make mistakes, they are not afraid to express opinions to know if it stands up to the perspectives of others. Moreover, they enjoy knowing that they are wrong when they learn something from it.

Take advantage of opportunities

When self-confident people see opportunities they take the bull by the horns, they don't worry about whether it will go badly or not, they wonder if something could stop them and they go for success. It's not that they are afraid, it's that they don't let anything stop them.

They celebrate others achievements

Someone who is unsure of himself doubts his relevance and therefore steals his camera to speak ill of others, to feel a little courage. Confident people do not care about their relevance, they know that values are innate and they see the wonderful things that other people offer them.

They're not afraid to ask for help

A person who is really sure of himself knows when it is time to ask for help, he does not feel weak so he is not ignorant either. They know their strengths and weaknesses well and support others when they know they lack a necessary characteristic to achieve something. They know that learning from someone else who has more experience is a way to improve.

Conclusion

We have reached the end of this journey where we have seen the strategies needed to achieve security. Remember that security is not the same as the ego, when a person feels powerfully protected by the ego, it is nothing more than a mask that is put on to hide all the fears he has.

Security is feeling good about yourself, accepting the good things, your talents and gifts, as well as accepting the weaknesses you have, the shortcomings and even the fears that each of us faces.

When we manage to reach this level, we already have a good path and we begin to recognize how to gain security or at least how to begin to develop it.

After knowing ourselves a little more and accepting ourselves, we have to work on all the limiting beliefs, know them, look for them in every corner of our mind, confront them and start to take them out or transform them into something better for ourselves.

In the moment in which we recognize that limiting belief, we stick it to the corner, take it and discover where it was born, we must make an introspection to rationalize it and realize its veracity. Right at that moment is where we can start working on it.

Because they are the anchors that are handled in neurolinguistic programming, a fact of the past that has filled us with beliefs that without realizing, limits us.

Although it will be impossible not to achieve throughout life beliefs that limit, we can stop them and start working to control them.

We will be able to build a more reliable model of reality for ourselves and we will know how to stop catching it from the outside and think for ourselves.

When we have managed to get to know ourselves with our securities and deficiencies, with our limiting beliefs and gifts, then we can work on developing skills that give us security and allow us to become more self-confident people.

For example, getting incentives in the work that make us feel good; developing full attention through different techniques or practicing some martial art or learning to dance, these last two widely proven to be ideal to increase self-confidence.

Although we should not only focus on our inner part, which is extremely important, but also on our outer part. Having said that, we have to take care of our image, first for ourselves, because we are the ones who feel happy when we walk around dressed in clothes that fit us and that enhance our attributes. But also for others, who see our presence and feel a better vibration than when they see us dressed in a disheveled look.

Then, when you have developed self-confidence, or are in the process of development, then don't miss the opportunity to become independent, not only from your parents' house or from the space you are in, but even to become independent from yourself, leaving behind all those fears, worries, and throwing yourself into achieving all the dreams you have in the inkwell.

Remember that this can be translated as leaving the comfort zone. The first requirement to work on when developing this skill is that we can develop the strength to break out of that comfortable comfort zone that keeps us tied down for years to come.

When you break all the chains and go out and eat the world, we come to the end, which is one of those chains that binds many around the world: what people might say.

For you to develop the best security of all, you have to leave behind those fears and those insecurities and especially forget what they will say. The consequences of your actions, what you don't achieve and what you do achieve, will only be enjoyed or suffered by you. No one else.

Leave behind the fear of rejection, of what others may say, and do whatever you want to do to achieve the glory and the goals you want to achieve in your life.

In your hands is the power to achieve what you want.